Praying
Through the
BIBLE

A PRAYER
JOURNAL

STORMIE
OMARTIAN

HARVEST HOUSE PUBLISHERS

EUGENE, OREGON

PRAYING THROUGH THE BIBLE
Copyright © 2007 by Stormie Omartian
Published by Harvest House Publishers
Eugene, Oregon 97402
www.harvesthousepublishers.com

ISBN-13: 978-0-7369-2087-2
ISBN-10: 0-7369-2087-0

Printed in the United States of America

07 08 09 10 11 12 13 14 15 / VP-CF / 10 9 8 7 6 5 4 3 2

$\mathcal{S}$peak to My Heart, Lord...

✣

Our personal experiences in the Word of God are valuable and worth writing about. That's why whenever I read the Bible, I always try to have with me a pen and a notebook—or a journal such as this—so I can write down whatever I feel the Lord is speaking to my heart from His Word. I also find that each time I read the Scriptures I am inspired to pray about things in my life or in the world around me that I might not have thought of otherwise, and I want to write out some of those prayers—just like writing a letter to God.

As you spend time in God's Word, I encourage you to use this journal to record your insights and thoughts. When you choose the book, chapter, and verses you want to read, jot down that reference on the line provided at the top of the blank lines on each page. Then write out what God is speaking to your heart and how you feel inspired to pray. Include prayers for your own life and the situations that concern you. Write as little or as much as you want.

At the bottom of each page I have added a short prayer of my own inspired by a specific passage of God's Word. I hope it will inspire you to pray from Scripture too. When you let God's Word inspire your prayers, you learn to read the Bible *prayerfully* and to pray *scripturally*. And that's powerful. I know that once you start writing in this journal, you won't want to stop until you have filled every page with private words you will visit again and again in the years to come.

Stormie Omartian

This is what I'm led to pray as I read God's Word today.

The Scripture I have read is _____.

_____

_____

_____

_____

_____

_____

_____

_____

_____

_____

_____

_____

_____

_____

_____

_____

_____

Thank You, Lord, for
Your beautiful creation. I worship You
as my Creator and thank You
for creating me in Your image.

GENESIS 1:1-27

This is what I'm led to pray as I read God's Word today.

The Scripture I have read is _____.

_____

_____

_____

_____

_____

_____

_____

_____

_____

_____

_____

_____

_____

_____

_____

_____

_____

God, help me to obey You
at all times and never assume
that I know what's best for my life.

GENESIS 3:1-13

This is what I'm led to pray as I read God's Word today.

The Scripture I have read is _____.

_____

_____

_____

_____

_____

_____

_____

_____

_____

_____

_____

_____

_____

_____

_____

_____

Heavenly Father,

show me how to worship You the way
You want me to so that I will always
have a close relationship with You.

GENESIS 4:1-16

This is what I'm led to pray as I read God's Word today.

The Scripture I have read is _____.

_____

_____

_____

_____

_____

_____

_____

_____

_____

_____

_____

_____

_____

_____

_____

_____

_____

_____

Dear God, enable
me to hear Your voice guiding me so
that I can do great things for You.

GENESIS 6:13-22

This is what I'm led to pray as I read God's Word today.

The Scripture I have read is _____.

_____

_____

_____

_____

_____

_____

_____

_____

_____

_____

_____

_____

_____

_____

_____

_____

Thank You, God,
for always keeping Your promises to me.

GENESIS 9:11

This is what I'm led to pray as I read God's Word today.

The Scripture I have read is _____.

Lord, show me how
to use the gifts and abilities You
have given me to bring glory to
Your name and not to myself.

GENESIS 11:4-9

This is what I'm led to pray as I read God's Word today.

The Scripture I have read is _____.

_____

_____

_____

_____

_____

_____

_____

_____

_____

_____

_____

_____

_____

_____

_____

_____

_____

Holy Father, may I
be like Abraham and always follow
You wherever You want me to go.

GENESIS 12:1-8

This is what I'm led to pray as I read God's Word today.

The Scripture I have read is _____.

_____

_____

_____

_____

_____

_____

_____

_____

_____

_____

_____

_____

_____

_____

_____

_____

_____

_____

Lord, guide me so that
I never end up living outside Your
best for me by choosing what I think
is best instead of asking You.

GENESIS 13:10-13

This is what I'm led to pray as I read God's Word today.

The Scripture I have read is _____.

_____

_____

_____

_____

_____

_____

_____

_____

_____

_____

_____

_____

_____

_____

_____

_____

_____

Help me, Lord, to trust in Your promises and not try to make things happen my own way.

GENESIS 16:1-5

This is what I'm led to pray as I read God's Word today.

The Scripture I have read is _____.

Dear God, strengthen my faith so I will always believe that nothing is too hard for You.

GENESIS 18:9-15

This is what I'm led to pray as I read God's Word today.

The Scripture I have read is _____.

_____

_____

_____

_____

_____

_____

_____

_____

_____

_____

_____

_____

_____

_____

_____

_____

Lord, give me the words to
pray boldly for the lives of others and not
give up or stop interceding too soon.

GENESIS 18:20-33

This is what I'm led to pray as I read God's Word today.

The Scripture I have read is _____.

_____

_____

_____

_____

_____

_____

_____

_____

_____

_____

_____

_____

_____

_____

_____

_____

_____

Dear Lord, walk
with me to where You are leading me;
help me to not keep looking back to the
past so that I become paralyzed by it.

GENESIS 19:22-29

This is what I'm led to pray as I read God's Word today.

The Scripture I have read is _____.

_____

_____

_____

_____

_____

_____

_____

_____

_____

_____

_____

_____

_____

_____

My precious Lord,
I thank You that when I cry out to
You in the dry and thirsty times of my
life, You will open my eyes to Your
provision of living water for me.
GENESIS 21:14-19

This is what I'm led to pray as I read God's Word today.

The Scripture I have read is _____.

_____

_____

_____

_____

_____

_____

_____

_____

_____

_____

_____

_____

_____

_____

_____

_____

_____

Heavenly Father,
help me to lay down all that I love so
that I can better serve all that *You* love.

GENESIS 22:2,9-12

This is what I'm led to pray as I read God's Word today.

The Scripture I have read is _____.

_____

Lord, give me self-control
so that I never succumb to the lust of
the flesh and end up losing the great
spiritual inheritance You have for me.

GENESIS 25:29-34

This is what I'm led to pray as I read God's Word today.

The Scripture I have read is _____.

_____
_____
_____
_____
_____
_____
_____
_____
_____
_____
_____
_____
_____
_____
_____
_____

Just as Jacob
heard Your voice when he was in the
middle of obeying You, Father, I pray
that I too will always obey You and
hear Your voice speaking to my heart.

GENESIS 28:10-15

This is what I'm led to pray as I read God's Word today.

The Scripture I have read is _____.

_____

_____

_____

_____

_____

_____

_____

_____

_____

_____

_____

_____

_____

_____

_____

God, I know when You get hold of our lives, we are never the same. Help me to continually surrender myself to You so that I can receive all that You have for me.

GENESIS 32:24-30

This is what I'm led to pray as I read God's Word today.

The Scripture I have read is _____.

_____

_____

_____

_____

_____

_____

_____

_____

_____

_____

_____

_____

_____

_____

_____

_____

God, remind me that even when
life seems unfair and things don't
turn out like I expect, You have a
plan for my life, and it is good.

GENESIS 37:23-35

This is what I'm led to pray as I read God's Word today.

The Scripture I have read is _____.

_____

_____

_____

_____

_____

_____

_____

_____

_____

_____

_____

_____

_____

_____

_____

_____

_____

Heavenly Father,

I thank You for the favor You show
to those who love, obey, and serve
You. Thank You for being with me
and making the things I do prosper.

GENESIS 39:20-23

This is what I'm led to pray as I read God's Word today.

The Scripture I have read is _____.

_____

_____

_____

_____

_____

_____

_____

_____

_____

_____

_____

_____

_____

_____

_____

_____

Lord, fill me so that I am
the type of person in whom people
will recognize Your Spirit.

GENESIS 41:38-43

This is what I'm led to pray as I read God's Word today.

The Scripture I have read is _____.

_____

_____

_____

_____

_____

_____

_____

_____

_____

_____

_____

_____

_____

_____

_____

God, make me a forgiving person just as Joseph was. Help me not to keep an account of wrongs against me but rather to see the bigger picture through Your eyes.

GENESIS 45:4-8

This is what I'm led to pray as I read God's Word today.

The Scripture I have read is _____.

_____

_____

_____

_____

_____

_____

_____

_____

_____

_____

_____

_____

_____

_____

_____

_____

_____

Lord, I thank You that
You take the evil that we experience
and use it for good. Help me to
see Your good in every situation.

GENESIS 50:15-21

This is what I'm led to pray as I read God's Word today.

The Scripture I have read is _____.

_____

_____

_____

_____

_____

_____

_____

_____

_____

_____

_____

_____

_____

_____

_____

Thank You,

Lord, for hearing my cry for
deliverance and rescuing me.

EXODUS 2:24

This is what I'm led to pray as I read God's Word today.

The Scripture I have read is _____.

_____

_____

_____

_____

_____

_____

_____

_____

_____

_____

_____

_____

_____

_____

_____

Lord, help me to walk so
closely with You that I can always hear
Your voice speaking to my heart.

EXODUS 3:4

This is what I'm led to pray as I read God's Word today.

The Scripture I have read is _____.

_____

_____

_____

_____

_____

_____

_____

_____

_____

_____

_____

_____

_____

_____

_____

Dear God, help me
to trust You completely whenever
I am hesitant to move out into
what You have called me to do.

EXODUS 4:10-17

This is what I'm led to pray as I read God's Word today.

The Scripture I have read is _____.

_____

_____

_____

_____

_____

_____

_____

_____

_____

_____

_____

_____

_____

_____

_____

_____

Heavenly Father,
help me to not be afraid to boldly deliver
Your message to whoever needs to hear it.

EXODUS 7:16

This is what I'm led to pray as I read God's Word today.

The Scripture I have read is _____.

_____

_____

_____

_____

_____

_____

_____

_____

_____

_____

_____

_____

_____

Dear God, help me to not be afraid in the face of my enemies, but rather to trust that You will fight the battles for me.

EXODUS 14:13-14

This is what I'm led to pray as I read God's Word today.

The Scripture I have read is _____.

_____

_____

_____

_____

_____

_____

_____

_____

_____

_____

_____

_____

_____

_____

_____

Thank You, Lord,
for being my Healer.

EXODUS 15:26

This is what I'm led to pray as I read God's Word today.

The Scripture I have read is _____.

_____

_____

_____

_____

_____

_____

_____

_____

_____

_____

_____

_____

_____

_____

_____

_____

Father God, write Your commandments on the tablets of my heart so that I will always remember to obey them.

EXODUS 20:1-17

This is what I'm led to pray as I read God's Word today.

The Scripture I have read is _____.

_____

_____

_____

_____

_____

_____

_____

_____

_____

_____

_____

_____

_____

_____

_____

_____

Lord, thank You for
blessing my food and water and
protecting me from sickness.

EXODUS 23:25-30

This is what I'm led to pray as I read God's Word today.

The Scripture I have read is _____.

_____

_____

_____

_____

_____

_____

_____

_____

_____

_____

_____

_____

_____

God, show me if I have lifted up my
heart to any kind of idol in my life so that
I may cast it down and destroy its hold.

EXODUS 32:7-9

This is what I'm led to pray as I read God's Word today.

The Scripture I have read is _____.

_____

_____

_____

_____

_____

_____

_____

_____

_____

_____

_____

_____

_____

_____

_____

_____

_____

_____

_____

Heavenly Father,
I don't want to go anywhere if Your
presence does not go with me.

EXODUS 33:13-15

This is what I'm led to pray as I read God's Word today.

The Scripture I have read is _____.

_____

_____

_____

_____

_____

_____

_____

_____

_____

_____

_____

_____

_____

_____

_____

_____

Thank You, Lord,
for always being merciful, gracious,
patient, and full of goodness and truth.

EXODUS 34:6-7

This is what I'm led to pray as I read God's Word today.

The Scripture I have read is _____.

Lord, reveal to me any way
that I have not obeyed Your laws so
that I may confess it to You as sin.

LEVITICUS 5:17

This is what I'm led to pray as I read God's Word today.

The Scripture I have read is _____.

_____

_____

_____

_____

_____

_____

_____

_____

_____

_____

_____

_____

_____

_____

_____

_____

_____

Lord, enable me to
be holy just as You are holy.

LEVITICUS 20:26

This is what I'm led to pray as I read God's Word today.

The Scripture I have read is _____.

_____

_____

_____

_____

_____

_____

_____

_____

_____

_____

_____

_____

_____

_____

_____

_____

_____

_____

Almighty God, I confess
my sins to You and ask that You would
forgive me and lead me in Your way.

LEVITICUS 26:40-44

This is what I'm led to pray as I read God's Word today.

The Scripture I have read is _____.

_____

_____

_____

_____

_____

_____

_____

_____

_____

_____

_____

_____

_____

_____

_____

_____

_____

_____

Lord, I pray that I will not
be a complaining person and that I
will have a heart filled with praise
and thanksgiving at all times.

NUMBERS 11:1

This is what I'm led to pray as I read God's Word today.

The Scripture I have read is _____.

_____

_____

_____

_____

_____

_____

_____

_____

_____

_____

_____

_____

_____

_____

_____

_____

Help me, Lord, to remember
to pray often on behalf of others.

NUMBERS 14:19-20

This is what I'm led to pray as I read God's Word today.

The Scripture I have read is _____.

_____

_____

_____

_____

_____

_____

_____

_____

_____

_____

_____

_____

_____

_____

_____

_____

_____

Heavenly Father,
open my eyes to always see the truth
about myself and my situation.

NUMBERS 22:31-34

This is what I'm led to pray as I read God's Word today.

The Scripture I have read is _____.

_____

_____

_____

_____

_____

_____

_____

_____

_____

_____

_____

_____

_____

_____

_____

_____

_____

_____

Lord, help me to get rid of
everything in my life that is offensive to
You so that it will not be a stumbling block.

NUMBERS 33:55

This is what I'm led to pray as I read God's Word today.

The Scripture I have read is _____.

_____

_____

_____

_____

_____

_____

_____

_____

_____

_____

_____

_____

_____

_____

Help me to always listen to
You, Lord, and not rebelliously assume
that I know the right thing to do.

DEUTERONOMY 1:43-45

This is what I'm led to pray as I read God's Word today.

The Scripture I have read is _____.

_____

_____

_____

_____

_____

_____

_____

_____

_____

_____

_____

_____

_____

_____

_____

_____

_____

Thank You, God, that
You will bring me out of hard places
with Your presence and Your power.

DEUTERONOMY 4:37-40

This is what I'm led to pray as I read God's Word today.

The Scripture I have read is _____.

_____

_____

_____

_____

_____

_____

_____

_____

_____

_____

_____

_____

_____

_____

_____

Thank You, holy
Father, for taking all sickness
and disease away from me.

DEUTERONOMY 7:15

This is what I'm led to pray as I read God's Word today.

The Scripture I have read is _____.

_____
_____
_____
_____
_____
_____
_____
_____
_____
_____
_____
_____
_____
_____
_____
_____
_____

Lord, help me not to
be weakened by sin, but to do all
You ask me to do so I can possess
all that You have for me.

DEUTERONOMY 11:8-14

This is what I'm led to pray as I read God's Word today.

The Scripture I have read is _____.

_____

_____

_____

_____

_____

_____

_____

_____

_____

_____

_____

_____

_____

_____

_____

_____

_____

_____

Dear God, show me
when, what, and to whom I need to give.

DEUTERONOMY 15:10

This is what I'm led to pray as I read God's Word today.

The Scripture I have read is _____.

_____

_____

_____

_____

_____

_____

_____

_____

_____

_____

_____

_____

_____

_____

_____

_____

_____

_____

Thank You, Almighty
God, that I don't have to be afraid when I
face opposition from the enemy because
You go with me to fight the battle.

DEUTERONOMY 20:1-4

This is what I'm led to pray as I read God's Word today.

The Scripture I have read is _____.

_____

_____

_____

_____

_____

_____

_____

_____

_____

_____

_____

_____

_____

_____

_____

_____

_____

Father, I thank You
for all Your many blessings of
provision and safety to me.

DEUTERONOMY 28:1-10

This is what I'm led to pray as I read God's Word today.

The Scripture I have read is _____.

Thank You, God,
that You will not leave or forsake me.

DEUTERONOMY 31:6

This is what I'm led to pray as I read God's Word today.

The Scripture I have read is _____.

_____

_____

_____

_____

_____

_____

_____

_____

_____

_____

_____

_____

_____

_____

_____

_____

_____

Heavenly Father,
enable me to be strong and not
afraid, knowing that You are
with me wherever I go.

JOSHUA 1:9

This is what I'm led to pray as I read God's Word today.

The Scripture I have read is _____.

God, help me not to do just
what I think is right without asking
You what You want me to do.

JOSHUA 9:14

This is what I'm led to pray as I read God's Word today.

The Scripture I have read is _____.

_____

_____

_____

_____

_____

_____

_____

_____

_____

_____

_____

_____

_____

_____

_____

_____

Father God,

I love You with all my heart, and
I choose to serve You this day.

JOSHUA 24:14-16

This is what I'm led to pray as I read God's Word today.

The Scripture I have read is _____.

_____

_____

_____

_____

_____

_____

_____

_____

_____

_____

_____

_____

_____

_____

_____

_____

_____

Lord, help me to remember
that even though I feel weak, Your
presence with me makes me strong.

JUDGES 6:15-16

This is what I'm led to pray as I read God's Word today.

The Scripture I have read is _____ .

_____

_____

_____

_____

_____

_____

_____

_____

_____

_____

_____

_____

_____

_____

_____

_____

_____

Heavenly Father,

help me to obey You and to resist
temptation so that I may always
have the fullness of Your presence.

JUDGES 16:20

This is what I'm led to pray as I read God's Word today.

The Scripture I have read is _____.

_____

_____

_____

_____

_____

_____

_____

_____

_____

_____

_____

_____

_____

_____

_____

_____

God, I pray that You will help me
not to give up when I face obstacles, but
to keep praying until I have victory.

JUDGES 20:18-28

This is what I'm led to pray as I read God's Word today.

The Scripture I have read is _____.

_____

_____

_____

_____

_____

_____

_____

_____

_____

_____

_____

_____

_____

_____

_____

_____

_____

_____

Thank You, Lord, that
You will redeem all my difficult situations
and use them for Your purposes and glory.

RUTH 4:13-17

This is what I'm led to pray as I read God's Word today.

The Scripture I have read is _____.

_____

_____

_____

_____

_____

_____

_____

_____

_____

_____

_____

_____

_____

_____

_____

_____

_____

_____

Lord, help me to reject anything
that is an idol in my life and return
entirely to You with all of my heart.

1 SAMUEL 7:3

This is what I'm led to pray as I read God's Word today.

The Scripture I have read is _____.

_____

_____

_____

_____

_____

_____

_____

_____

_____

_____

_____

_____

_____

_____

_____

_____

_____

_____

Dear God, I thank You that even when I make wrong choices, You will still bless me if I turn to You and follow Your ways.

1 SAMUEL 12:20

This is what I'm led to pray as I read God's Word today.

The Scripture I have read is _____.

_____

_____

_____

_____

_____

_____

_____

_____

_____

_____

_____

_____

_____

_____

_____

_____

_____

Help me to always
obey You, Lord, and let no
rebelliousness be found in me.

1 SAMUEL 15:22-23

This is what I'm led to pray as I read God's Word today.

The Scripture I have read is _____.

_____

_____

_____

_____

_____

_____

_____

_____

_____

_____

_____

_____

_____

_____

_____

_____

Father God, help me to always remember to ask You about where I should go and what I should do, and not assume I know the answer.

I SAMUEL 23:4

This is what I'm led to pray as I read God's Word today.

The Scripture I have read is _____.

_____

_____

_____

_____

_____

_____

_____

_____

_____

_____

_____

_____

_____

_____

_____

_____

_____

Lord, help me to
remember to do as David did and
stop often to worship You.

2 SAMUEL 6:13-15

This is what I'm led to pray as I read God's Word today.

The Scripture I have read is _____.

_____

_____

_____

_____

_____

_____

_____

_____

_____

_____

_____

_____

_____

_____

_____

God, help me to reject temptations
to sin when they first cross my mind.

2 SAMUEL 11:1-5

This is what I'm led to pray as I read God's Word today.

The Scripture I have read is _____.

_____

_____

_____

_____

_____

_____

_____

_____

_____

_____

_____

_____

_____

_____

_____

_____

Heavenly Father,
please protect me from any kind of
violent assault, and keep me safe
from those who intend to do evil.

2 SAMUEL 13:12-16

This is what I'm led to pray as I read God's Word today.

The Scripture I have read is _____.

_____

_____

_____

_____

_____

_____

_____

_____

_____

_____

_____

_____

_____

_____

_____

_____

Lord, give me persistence
and perseverance in prayer until I see
my enemies defeated and destroyed.

2 SAMUEL 22:38-41

This is what I'm led to pray as I read God's Word today.

The Scripture I have read is _____.

_____

_____

_____

_____

_____

_____

_____

_____

_____

_____

_____

_____

_____

_____

_____

_____

_____

Lord, help me to walk in
Your ways and keep Your commands
so that I may prosper in all I do.

1 KINGS 2:3

This is what I'm led to pray as I read God's Word today.

The Scripture I have read is _____.

_____

_____

_____

_____

_____

_____

_____

_____

_____

_____

_____

_____

_____

_____

_____

Holy Father, I ask that
You would always give me the ability
to discern between good and evil.

1 KINGS 3:9

This is what I'm led to pray as I read God's Word today.

The Scripture I have read is _____.

_____

_____

_____

_____

_____

_____

_____

_____

_____

_____

_____

_____

_____

_____

_____

_____

_____

_____

Lord, help me to be strong
and obey You regardless of how much
I may be enticed to do otherwise.

1 KINGS 13:6-10

This is what I'm led to pray as I read God's Word today.

The Scripture I have read is _____.

_____

_____

_____

_____

_____

_____

_____

_____

_____

_____

_____

_____

_____

_____

_____

_____

Give me the ability to
recognize any idols in my life, Lord,
and help me to remove them.

1 KINGS 15:11-12

This is what I'm led to pray as I read God's Word today.

The Scripture I have read is _____.

_____

_____

_____

_____

_____

_____

_____

_____

_____

_____

_____

_____

_____

_____

_____

_____

_____

_____

Lord, enlarge my heart
to contain all You have for me.

2 KINGS 4:1-6

This is what I'm led to pray as I read God's Word today.

The Scripture I have read is _____.

_____

_____

_____

_____

_____

_____

_____

_____

_____

_____

_____

_____

_____

_____

_____

_____

_____

Lord, open my eyes to
see the truth in all situations.

2 KINGS 6:16-17

This is what I'm led to pray as I read God's Word today.

The Scripture I have read is _____.

_____

_____

_____

_____

_____

_____

_____

_____

_____

_____

_____

_____

_____

_____

_____

_____

_____

_____

_____

Thank You, Lord, that
because I fear You, You will deliver
me from the hands of my enemies.

2 KINGS 17:39

This is what I'm led to pray as I read God's Word today.

The Scripture I have read is _____.

_____

_____

_____

_____

_____

_____

_____

_____

_____

_____

_____

_____

_____

_____

_____

_____

How grateful I am,
Lord, that You hear my prayers when
I am in a life-and-death situation.

2 KINGS 20:1-5

This is what I'm led to pray as I read God's Word today.

The Scripture I have read is _____.

_____

_____

_____

_____

_____

_____

_____

_____

_____

_____

_____

_____

_____

_____

_____

_____

_____

I long to follow You
with all my heart, Lord, and to obey
You to the very best of my ability.

2 KINGS 23:3

This is what I'm led to pray as I read God's Word today.

The Scripture I have read is _____.

_____

_____

_____

_____

_____

_____

_____

_____

_____

_____

_____

_____

_____

_____

_____

_____

God, bless me and enlarge
my sphere of influence; be with
me and deliver me from evil.

1 CHRONICLES 4:10

This is what I'm led to pray as I read God's Word today.

The Scripture I have read is _____.

_____

_____

_____

_____

_____

_____

_____

_____

_____

_____

_____

_____

_____

_____

_____

_____

_____

_____

_____

_____

God, help me to always seek
You and not any ungodly source.

1 CHRONICLES 10:13-14

This is what I'm led to pray as I read God's Word today.

The Scripture I have read is _____.

_____

_____

_____

_____

_____

_____

_____

_____

_____

_____

_____

_____

_____

_____

_____

_____

_____

_____

Thank You, Lord, that
when I am confronted by the enemy,
You will go before me into battle.

1 CHRONICLES 14:14-15

This is what I'm led to pray as I read God's Word today.

The Scripture I have read is _____.

_____

_____

_____

_____

_____

_____

_____

_____

_____

_____

_____

_____

_____

_____

_____

_____

_____

_____

I give thanks
to You, Lord, for filling my heart
with joy every time I seek You.

1 CHRONICLES 16:8-12

This is what I'm led to pray as I read God's Word today.

The Scripture I have read is _____.

_____

_____

_____

_____

_____

_____

_____

_____

_____

_____

_____

_____

_____

_____

_____

_____

_____

Lord, I don't want to offer
anything to You that costs me nothing.

1 CHRONICLES 21:24

This is what I'm led to pray as I read God's Word today.

The Scripture I have read is _____.

_____

_____

_____

_____

_____

_____

_____

_____

_____

_____

_____

_____

_____

_____

Help me to do something
great for You, Lord.

2 CHRONICLES 2:1

This is what I'm led to pray as I read God's Word today.

The Scripture I have read is _____.

_____

_____

_____

_____

_____

_____

_____

_____

_____

_____

_____

_____

_____

_____

_____

_____

Lord, I humble myself before
You and pray that You would forgive the
sins of my people and heal our land.

2 CHRONICLES 7:14

This is what I'm led to pray as I read God's Word today.

The Scripture I have read is _____.

_____

_____

_____

_____

_____

_____

_____

_____

_____

_____

_____

_____

_____

_____

_____

_____

_____

_____

_____

Reward the work
of my hands with success, Lord.

2 CHRONICLES 15:7

This is what I'm led to pray as I read God's Word today.

The Scripture I have read is _____.

_____

_____

_____

_____

_____

_____

_____

_____

_____

_____

_____

_____

_____

_____

_____

_____

Help me
to speak only Your truth, Lord.

2 CHRONICLES 18:13

This is what I'm led to pray as I read God's Word today.

The Scripture I have read is _____.

Thank You
that the battles I face are Yours, Lord.

2 CHRONICLES 20:15

This is what I'm led to pray as I read God's Word today.

The Scripture I have read is _____.

_____

_____

_____

_____

_____

_____

_____

_____

_____

_____

_____

_____

_____

_____

_____

_____

_____

_____

Lord, I thank You for the solid
foundation You have laid in my life.

EZRA 3:11

This is what I'm led to pray as I read God's Word today.

The Scripture I have read is _____.

_____

_____

_____

_____

_____

_____

_____

_____

_____

_____

_____

_____

_____

_____

_____

_____

Thank You, Lord,
that Your hand is upon me and You will
deliver me from the hand of the enemy.

EZRA 8:31

This is what I'm led to pray as I read God's Word today.

The Scripture I have read is _____.

_____

_____

_____

_____

_____

_____

_____

_____

_____

_____

_____

_____

_____

_____

_____

Lord, help me to be
watchful in prayer so the enemy
cannot come in and undermine the
work You have given me to do.

NEHEMIAH 4:7-11

This is what I'm led to pray as I read God's Word today.

The Scripture I have read is _____.

_____

_____

_____

_____

_____

_____

_____

_____

_____

_____

_____

_____

_____

_____

_____

_____

_____

Enable me
to not succumb to fear, which I know is
part of Satan's plan for my destruction.

NEHEMIAH 6:9-11

This is what I'm led to pray as I read God's Word today.

The Scripture I have read is _____.

_____

_____

_____

_____

_____

_____

_____

_____

_____

_____

_____

_____

_____

_____

_____

_____

_____

Prepare me, Lord, for such
a time when I can be Your instrument
of salvation and deliverance for others.

ESTHER 4:13-17

This is what I'm led to pray as I read God's Word today.

The Scripture I have read is _____.

_____

_____

_____

_____

_____

_____

_____

_____

_____

_____

_____

_____

_____

_____

_____

_____

Lord, may I trust You in
the hard times with the same faith
as when things are going well.

JOB 13:15

This is what I'm led to pray as I read God's Word today.

The Scripture I have read is _____.

_____

_____

_____

_____

_____

_____

_____

_____

_____

_____

_____

_____

_____

_____

_____

_____

_____

Thank You, Lord, that
You know me, and You see everything I do.

JOB 31:4

This is what I'm led to pray as I read God's Word today.

The Scripture I have read is _____.

Lord, forgive me if I have ever
questioned Your ways or judgments.

JOB 40:8-14

This is what I'm led to pray as I read God's Word today.

The Scripture I have read is _____.

_____

_____

_____

_____

_____

_____

_____

_____

_____

_____

_____

_____

_____

_____

_____

Father God,

help me to forgive others when they
are thoughtless and lack compassion.

JOB 42:10

This is what I'm led to pray as I read God's Word today.

The Scripture I have read is _____.

_____

_____

_____

_____

_____

_____

_____

_____

_____

_____

_____

_____

_____

_____

_____

_____

_____

Thank You
for always hearing my prayer, Lord.

PSALM 6:8-9

This is what I'm led to pray as I read God's Word today.

The Scripture I have read is _____.

_____

_____

_____

_____

_____

_____

_____

_____

_____

_____

_____

_____

_____

_____

Lord, You are excellent
and worthy of all praise.

PSALM 8:1

This is what I'm led to pray as I read God's Word today.

The Scripture I have read is _____.

_____

_____

_____

_____

_____

_____

_____

_____

_____

_____

_____

_____

_____

_____

_____

_____

_____

Thank You, Lord,
for keeping me safe.

PSALM 12:5

This is what I'm led to pray as I read God's Word today.

The Scripture I have read is _____.

_____

_____

_____

_____

_____

_____

_____

_____

_____

_____

_____

_____

_____

_____

_____

_____

_____

Lord, how grateful I am that
You live in the praises of Your people.

PSALM 22:3

This is what I'm led to pray as I read God's Word today.

The Scripture I have read is _____.

_____

_____

_____

_____

_____

_____

_____

_____

_____

_____

_____

_____

_____

_____

_____

_____

_____

I pray that You,
Father, would restore my soul and lead
me on the path You have for my life.

PSALM 23:3

This is what I'm led to pray as I read God's Word today.

The Scripture I have read is _____.

_____

_____

_____

_____

_____

_____

_____

_____

_____

_____

_____

_____

_____

_____

_____

_____

Lord, show me any sin in my
life that needs to be confessed before
You so that my heart can be clean.

PSALM 32:1-5

This is what I'm led to pray as I read God's Word today.

The Scripture I have read is _____.

_____

_____

_____

_____

_____

_____

_____

_____

_____

_____

_____

_____

_____

_____

_____

_____

_____

_____

Thank You, heavenly
Father, for setting me free from all fear.

PSALM 34:4

This is what I'm led to pray as I read God's Word today.

The Scripture I have read is _____.

_____

_____

_____

_____

_____

_____

_____

_____

_____

_____

_____

_____

_____

_____

_____

_____

Lord, I refuse to be discouraged,
for I know my hope is in You.

PSALM 42:5

This is what I'm led to pray as I read God's Word today.

The Scripture I have read is _____.

_____

_____

_____

_____

_____

_____

_____

_____

_____

_____

_____

_____

_____

_____

_____

_____

_____

_____

Thank You, Lord, for
seeing my tears and knowing my situation.

PSALM 56:8-9

This is what I'm led to pray as I read God's Word today.

The Scripture I have read is _____.

_____

_____

_____

_____

_____

_____

_____

_____

_____

_____

_____

_____

_____

_____

_____

_____

Lord, keep my eyes from
ever looking at anything evil.

PSALM 101:3

This is what I'm led to pray as I read God's Word today.

The Scripture I have read is _____.

_____

_____

_____

_____

_____

_____

_____

_____

_____

_____

_____

_____

_____

_____

_____

_____

Thank You, Lord,
for delivering me out of darkness
and saving me from my distress.

PSALM 107:10-13

This is what I'm led to pray as I read God's Word today.

The Scripture I have read is _____.

_____

_____

_____

_____

_____

_____

_____

_____

_____

_____

_____

_____

_____

_____

_____

_____

_____

Father, I thank You that I
don't have to be afraid of bad news.

PSALM 112:6-8

This is what I'm led to pray as I read God's Word today.

The Scripture I have read is _____.

_____

_____

_____

_____

_____

_____

_____

_____

_____

_____

_____

_____

_____

_____

_____

_____

_____

_____

Help me to wait patiently
on You, Lord, for Your perfect
timing and answer to my prayers.

PSALM 130:5-6

This is what I'm led to pray as I read God's Word today.

The Scripture I have read is _____.

_____

_____

_____

_____

_____

_____

_____

_____

_____

_____

_____

_____

_____

_____

_____

_____

Put a guard
over my lips, Lord, so that I will never
say anything wrong or hurtful.

PSALM 141:3

This is what I'm led to pray as I read God's Word today.

The Scripture I have read is _____.

_____

_____

_____

_____

_____

_____

_____

_____

_____

_____

_____

_____

_____

_____

_____

_____

_____

Lord, give me wisdom
so that I may bless others and
live in joy and happiness.

PROVERBS 3:13-18

This is what I'm led to pray as I read God's Word today.

The Scripture I have read is _____.

_____

_____

_____

_____

_____

_____

_____

_____

_____

_____

_____

_____

_____

_____

_____

_____

_____

Bless me,
Lord, for I know that no sorrow
comes without Your blessing.

PROVERBS 10:22

This is what I'm led to pray as I read God's Word today.

The Scripture I have read is _____.

_____

_____

_____

_____

_____

_____

_____

_____

_____

_____

_____

_____

_____

_____

_____

_____

God, give me words that
speak life to people.

PROVERBS 18:21

This is what I'm led to pray as I read God's Word today.

The Scripture I have read is _____.

Lord, help me to rule
over my mind and emotions.

PROVERBS 25:28

This is what I'm led to pray as I read God's Word today.

The Scripture I have read is _____.

_____

_____

_____

_____

_____

_____

_____

_____

_____

_____

_____

_____

_____

_____

_____

_____

Lord, help me to be a woman
who fears You and finds favor in Your eyes.

PROVERBS 31:30

This is what I'm led to pray as I read God's Word today.

The Scripture I have read is _____.

_____

_____

_____

_____

_____

_____

_____

_____

_____

_____

_____

_____

_____

_____

_____

_____

Lord, help me to remember
that nothing is more important
in this life than knowing, serving,
obeying, and reverencing You.

ECCLESIASTES 12:13-14

This is what I'm led to pray as I read God's Word today.

The Scripture I have read is _____.

Teach me, Lord, to love
others the way that You love me.

SONG OF SONGS 8:6

This is what I'm led to pray as I read God's Word today.

The Scripture I have read is _____.

_____

_____

_____

_____

_____

_____

_____

_____

_____

_____

_____

_____

_____

_____

Dear God, may I never
fall into the confusion of the world
and become so wise in my own eyes
that I can see evil and call it good.

ISAIAH 5:20-21

This is what I'm led to pray as I read God's Word today.

The Scripture I have read is _____.

_____

_____

_____

_____

_____

_____

_____

_____

_____

_____

_____

_____

_____

_____

_____

_____

Thank You, Lord,
that when I am weary I can always
find rest and refreshment in You.

ISAIAH 28:12

This is what I'm led to pray as I read God's Word today.

The Scripture I have read is _____.

_____

_____

_____

_____

_____

_____

_____

_____

_____

_____

_____

_____

_____

_____

_____

_____

Help me, God, to live a righteous
life so that I may always dwell in a
peaceful, quiet, secure, and restful place.

ISAIAH 32:17-18

This is what I'm led to pray as I read God's Word today.

The Scripture I have read is _____.

_____

_____

_____

_____

_____

_____

_____

_____

_____

_____

_____

_____

_____

_____

_____

_____

_____

I pray that I can always walk
in the way of Your holiness, Lord, so
that I will obtain the joy and gladness
and safety You have for me there.

ISAIAH 35:8-10

This is what I'm led to pray as I read God's Word today.

The Scripture I have read is _____.

_____

_____

_____

_____

_____

_____

_____

_____

_____

_____

_____

_____

_____

_____

_____

Lord, I wait on You to renew
my strength so that I can rise up and run
the race and not become weary or weak.

ISAIAH 40:31

This is what I'm led to pray as I read God's Word today.

The Scripture I have read is _____ .

_____

_____

_____

_____

_____

_____

_____

_____

_____

_____

_____

_____

_____

_____

_____

_____

_____

Help me to always remember
that I belong to You, Lord, so
that I never forget who I am.

ISAIAH 44:5

This is what I'm led to pray as I read God's Word today.

The Scripture I have read is _____.

_____

_____

_____

_____

_____

_____

_____

_____

_____

_____

_____

_____

_____

_____

_____

_____

_____

_____

Thank You, Lord, that
You have borne my grief and sorrow,
You have paid the price for my sin, and
because of Your suffering I can be healed.

ISAIAH 53:4-5

This is what I'm led to pray as I read God's Word today.

The Scripture I have read is _____.

_____

_____

_____

_____

_____

_____

_____

_____

_____

_____

_____

_____

_____

_____

_____

_____

_____

Lord, I thank You for
hearing my prayers, and even before I
call, You have set Yourself to answer.

ISAIAH 65:24

This is what I'm led to pray as I read God's Word today.

The Scripture I have read is _____.

_____

_____

_____

_____

_____

_____

_____

_____

_____

_____

_____

_____

_____

_____

_____

_____

Lord, show me the path
You have for me so that I may walk
in it and find rest for my soul.

JEREMIAH 6:16

This is what I'm led to pray as I read God's Word today.

The Scripture I have read is _____.

Heavenly Father,
please keep me from committing
any kind of deception or
speaking anything but truth.

JEREMIAH 9:5-6

This is what I'm led to pray as I read God's Word today.

The Scripture I have read is _____.

_____

_____

_____

_____

_____

_____

_____

_____

_____

_____

_____

_____

_____

_____

_____

_____

Help me, God, to not just do what I want instead of listening to You and doing what You want.

JEREMIAH 16:11-13

This is what I'm led to pray as I read God's Word today.

The Scripture I have read is _____.

_____

_____

_____

_____

_____

_____

_____

_____

_____

_____

_____

_____

_____

_____

_____

_____

Lord, I pray that I will listen for
Your voice just as diligently when things
are going well as I do in the difficult times.

JEREMIAH 22:21

This is what I'm led to pray as I read God's Word today.

The Scripture I have read is _____.

_____

_____

_____

_____

_____

_____

_____

_____

_____

_____

_____

_____

_____

_____

_____

Dear God, help me to always turn to You with my whole heart and acknowledge that You are my Lord.

JEREMIAH 24:7

This is what I'm led to pray as I read God's Word today.

The Scripture I have read is _____.

Lord, help me to remember
all You have taught me in Your
Word and have spoken to me in
times of prayer and devotions.

JEREMIAH 30:2

This is what I'm led to pray as I read God's Word today.

The Scripture I have read is _____.

_____

_____

_____

_____

_____

_____

_____

_____

_____

_____

_____

_____

_____

_____

_____

_____

_____

I am grateful, Lord,
that You are the Creator of heaven
and earth, and because of Your
power, nothing is too hard for You.

JEREMIAH 32:17

This is what I'm led to pray as I read God's Word today.

The Scripture I have read is _____.

_____

_____

_____

_____

_____

_____

_____

_____

_____

_____

_____

_____

_____

_____

_____

_____

Lord, I thank You for
protecting those who trust in You
and who listen to You and obey.

JEREMIAH 39:17-18

This is what I'm led to pray as I read God's Word today.

The Scripture I have read is _____.

_____

_____

_____

_____

_____

_____

_____

_____

_____

_____

_____

_____

_____

Lord, I pray that I will
never do Your work in a deceitful
or lax way, but always in a spirit of
truth and devotion to serving You.

JEREMIAH 48:10

This is what I'm led to pray as I read God's Word today.

The Scripture I have read is _____.

_____

_____

_____

_____

_____

_____

_____

_____

_____

_____

_____

_____

_____

_____

_____

_____

Thank You, Lord,
that Your mercies to me are new every
morning, and Your love, faithfulness,
and compassion increasingly
strengthen my hope in You each day.
LAMENTATIONS 3:22-24

This is what I'm led to pray as I read God's Word today.

The Scripture I have read is _____.

_____

_____

_____

_____

_____

_____

_____

_____

_____

_____

_____

_____

_____

_____

_____

Thank You, Lord, that because of Jesus living in me, You do not judge me according to what I deserve.

EZEKIEL 7:27

This is what I'm led to pray as I read God's Word today.

The Scripture I have read is _____.

_____

_____

_____

_____

_____

_____

_____

_____

_____

_____

_____

_____

_____

_____

_____

Help me, Lord, to never
speak a word that is not from You
or share a vision that is strictly from
my own heart and not from Yours.

EZEKIEL 13:7

This is what I'm led to pray as I read God's Word today.

The Scripture I have read is _____.

_____

_____

_____

_____

_____

_____

_____

_____

_____

_____

_____

_____

_____

_____

_____

Dear God, I ask You
to keep my heart from ever trusting in
the good things You give me instead of
trusting in You, the Giver of all that I have.

EZEKIEL 16:14-15

This is what I'm led to pray as I read God's Word today.

The Scripture I have read is _____.

_____

_____

_____

_____

_____

_____

_____

_____

_____

_____

_____

_____

_____

_____

_____

_____

Lord, help me to never get so
full of myself and what I have that I fail
to share it with the poor and needy.

EZEKIEL 16:49

This is what I'm led to pray as I read God's Word today.

The Scripture I have read is _____.

_____

_____

_____

_____

_____

_____

_____

_____

_____

_____

_____

_____

_____

_____

Heavenly Father,

I pray for people in my own community
who have set themselves to do evil,
that they would turn from their
wicked ways and serve only You.

EZEKIEL 33:9

This is what I'm led to pray as I read God's Word today.

The Scripture I have read is _____.

_____

_____

_____

_____

_____

_____

_____

_____

_____

_____

_____

_____

_____

_____

_____

_____

I pray that I will never hear
Your Word and not do it, Lord, or
speak words of love to You while at the
same time pursuing my own gain.

EZEKIEL 33:31

This is what I'm led to pray as I read God's Word today.

The Scripture I have read is _____.

_____

_____

_____

_____

_____

_____

_____

_____

_____

_____

_____

_____

_____

_____

_____

Lord, keep my mouth from
ever profaning Your name in any way
and help me to make known the glory
of Your holy name wherever I go.

EZEKIEL 39:7

This is what I'm led to pray as I read God's Word today.

The Scripture I have read is _____.

Thank You, Lord,
for making me to be a temple in
which Your Holy Spirit dwells.

EZEKIEL 43:7

This is what I'm led to pray as I read God's Word today.

The Scripture I have read is _____.

_____

_____

_____

_____

_____

_____

_____

_____

_____

_____

_____

_____

_____

_____

_____

_____

Lord, may I continually
produce the fruit of Your Spirit because
of the edifying and healing stream of
living water flowing from You into me.

EZEKIEL 47:12

This is what I'm led to pray as I read God's Word today.

The Scripture I have read is _____.

_____

_____

_____

_____

_____

_____

_____

_____

_____

_____

_____

_____

_____

_____

_____

God, help me to always have
a sense of my own destiny and not
let the world affect my identity or
compromise my purpose in any way.

DANIEL 1:7-8

This is what I'm led to pray as I read God's Word today.

The Scripture I have read is _____.

_____

_____

_____

_____

_____

_____

_____

_____

_____

_____

_____

_____

_____

_____

_____

Thank You, Jesus, that
when the heat is on in our lives, You
get in the fire with us and are faithful
to those who are faithful to You.

DANIEL 3:25

This is what I'm led to pray as I read God's Word today.

The Scripture I have read is _____.

_____

_____

_____

_____

_____

_____

_____

_____

_____

_____

_____

_____

_____

_____

_____

_____

Lord, give me wisdom,
shine Your light through me, and
enable me to lead many to You.

DANIEL 12:3

This is what I'm led to pray as I read God's Word today.

The Scripture I have read is _____.

_____

_____

_____

_____

_____

_____

_____

_____

_____

_____

_____

_____

_____

_____

_____

_____

_____

Lord, give me wisdom and
knowledge so that I will not do things
in ignorance and perish because of it.

HOSEA 4:6

This is what I'm led to pray as I read God's Word today.

The Scripture I have read is _____.

_____

_____

_____

_____

_____

_____

_____

_____

_____

_____

_____

_____

_____

_____

_____

_____

Heavenly Father,
I pray that my soul will never experience
the famine of not hearing Your words
to my heart or the drought of not having
a fresh flow of Your Spirit in my life.

AMOS 8:11

This is what I'm led to pray as I read God's Word today.

The Scripture I have read is _____.

_____

_____

_____

_____

_____

_____

_____

_____

_____

_____

_____

_____

_____

_____

_____

_____

Lord, help me to never run from what You are instructing me to do, but thank You that if I were to do that, You are a God of second chances.

JONAH 3:1

This is what I'm led to pray as I read God's Word today.

The Scripture I have read is _____.

_____

_____

_____

_____

_____

_____

_____

_____

_____

_____

_____

_____

_____

_____

_____

_____

_____

Heavenly Father,
I pray that I will never cause distance
or separation between You and me
by doing anything that would be
considered evil in Your sight.
MICAH 3:4

This is what I'm led to pray as I read God's Word today.

The Scripture I have read is _____.

_____

_____

_____

_____

_____

_____

_____

_____

_____

_____

_____

_____

_____

_____

_____

Thank You, Lord, that
You are a refuge in times of trouble and
that You love all who trust in You.

NAHUM 1:7

This is what I'm led to pray as I read God's Word today.

The Scripture I have read is _____.

_____

_____

_____

_____

_____

_____

_____

_____

_____

_____

_____

_____

_____

_____

_____

_____

_____

_____

Lord, show me anything in my
life that has become an idol to me, and
reveal whatever has captured my heart
more than You, and I will bow before
You in repentance and reverence.

HABAKKUK 2:18-20

This is what I'm led to pray as I read God's Word today.

The Scripture I have read is _____.

_____

_____

_____

_____

_____

_____

_____

_____

_____

_____

_____

_____

_____

_____

_____

Heavenly Father,
I humble myself before You and seek
Your face and Your righteousness
this day, and I ask that I will always
have the courage to do what's right.
ZEPHANIAH 2:3

This is what I'm led to pray as I read God's Word today.

The Scripture I have read is _____.

_____

_____

_____

_____

_____

_____

_____

_____

_____

_____

_____

_____

_____

_____

_____

_____

_____

_____

Lord, You are my stronghold,
and I thank You for restoring double to
me of all that has been lost in my life.

ZECHARIAH 9:12

This is what I'm led to pray as I read God's Word today.

The Scripture I have read is _____.

_____

_____

_____

_____

_____

_____

_____

_____

_____

_____

_____

_____

_____

_____

Heavenly Father,

I thank You that because my
hope is in You, You will continue
to refine and purify me.

ZECHARIAH 13:9

This is what I'm led to pray as I read God's Word today.

The Scripture I have read is _____.

_____

_____

_____

_____

_____

_____

_____

_____

_____

_____

_____

_____

_____

_____

_____

_____

_____

God, help me to never rob You of the
tithes and offerings I owe You, and thank
You for opening up the windows of heaven
and pouring out Your blessing upon me.

MALACHI 3:8-11

This is what I'm led to pray as I read God's Word today.

The Scripture I have read is _____.

_____

_____

_____

_____

_____

_____

_____

_____

_____

_____

_____

_____

_____

_____

_____

Heavenly Father,

I repent of all my sins before You,
because I know that repentance
prepares the way in my heart for You
to do Your perfect work in me.

MATTHEW 3:1-3

This is what I'm led to pray as I read God's Word today.

The Scripture I have read is _____.

Lord, help me to feed on Your
Word daily so that I will never hunger
after things that do not give life.

MATTHEW 4:4

This is what I'm led to pray as I read God's Word today.

The Scripture I have read is _____.

_____

_____

_____

_____

_____

_____

_____

_____

_____

_____

_____

_____

_____

_____

_____

_____

Jesus, help me to have big faith
so that I can pray to You, believing that
You will calm the storms in my life.

MATTHEW 8:26

This is what I'm led to pray as I read God's Word today.

The Scripture I have read is _____.

_____

_____

_____

_____

_____

_____

_____

_____

_____

_____

_____

_____

_____

_____

_____

_____

_____

Dear Jesus,
give me courage so that I will never
deny You in any way, regardless of
the circumstances I may face.

MATTHEW 10:32-33

This is what I'm led to pray as I read God's Word today.

The Scripture I have read is _____.

_____

_____

_____

_____

_____

_____

_____

_____

_____

_____

_____

_____

_____

_____

_____

_____

_____

Lord, give me the kind of faith
that can move mountains in my life.

MATTHEW 17:20

This is what I'm led to pray as I read God's Word today.

The Scripture I have read is _____.

_____

_____

_____

_____

_____

_____

_____

_____

_____

_____

_____

_____

_____

_____

_____

_____

_____

_____

Thank You, Lord, that
with You all things are possible and
I can face the seemingly impossible
situations in my life with faith and hope.

MATTHEW 19:26

This is what I'm led to pray as I read God's Word today.

The Scripture I have read is _____.

_____

_____

_____

_____

_____

_____

_____

_____

_____

_____

_____

_____

_____

_____

_____

_____

_____

Father God, enable me to always be faithful over everything You entrust to my care so that I may enter into the fullness of joy found in You.

MATTHEW 25:21

This is what I'm led to pray as I read God's Word today.

The Scripture I have read is _____.

Precious Jesus,
thank You that You died and rose again for
me so that I may have life forever in You.

MATTHEW 28:5-6

This is what I'm led to pray as I read God's Word today.

The Scripture I have read is _____.

_____

_____

_____

_____

_____

_____

_____

_____

_____

_____

_____

_____

_____

_____

_____

Lord, enable me to
understand what I hear from You
and apply it to my life so that my
spiritual understanding will grow.

MARK 4:24-25

This is what I'm led to pray as I read God's Word today.

The Scripture I have read is _____.

_____

_____

_____

_____

_____

_____

_____

_____

_____

_____

_____

_____

_____

_____

_____

_____

Lord, remove anything that
keeps me from loving You with all
my heart, soul, mind, and strength.

MARK 12:30

This is what I'm led to pray as I read God's Word today.

The Scripture I have read is _____.

_____

_____

_____

_____

_____

_____

_____

_____

_____

_____

_____

_____

_____

_____

_____

_____

Dear Jesus,
keep me undeceived so that I will
not listen to any false teaching or
believe any lies of the enemy.

MARK 13:21-22

This is what I'm led to pray as I read God's Word today.

The Scripture I have read is _____.

_____

_____

_____

_____

_____

_____

_____

_____

_____

_____

_____

_____

_____

_____

_____

_____

Father, keep me watchful
and prayerful so that I do not enter
into any kind of temptation.

MARK 14:38

This is what I'm led to pray as I read God's Word today.

The Scripture I have read is _____.

_____

_____

_____

_____

_____

_____

_____

_____

_____

_____

_____

_____

_____

_____

_____

Jesus, I ask that You would give me the power to lay hands on the sick and pray in Your name for them to be healed and see them recover as You answer that prayer.

MARK 16:18

This is what I'm led to pray as I read God's Word today.

The Scripture I have read is _____.

_____

_____

_____

_____

_____

_____

_____

_____

_____

_____

_____

_____

_____

_____

_____

_____

_____

_____

Jesus, help me to be like
You—always aware that I need to
be about my Father's business.

LUKE 2:49

This is what I'm led to pray as I read God's Word today.

The Scripture I have read is _____ .

_____

_____

_____

_____

_____

_____

_____

_____

_____

_____

_____

_____

_____

_____

Lord, help me to continually
resist the lies and temptations of
the enemy with the knowledge
and power of Your Word.

LUKE 4:3-4

This is what I'm led to pray as I read God's Word today.

The Scripture I have read is _____.

_____

_____

_____

_____

_____

_____

_____

_____

_____

_____

_____

_____

_____

_____

_____

_____

Heavenly Father,
fill my heart with the knowledge and
remembrance of Your Word so that I
only speak out of the abundance of a
heart saturated with Your truth.

LUKE 6:45

This is what I'm led to pray as I read God's Word today.

The Scripture I have read is _____.

_____

_____

_____

_____

_____

_____

_____

_____

_____

_____

_____

_____

_____

_____

_____

_____

Father, help me to always stay
on the narrow path of life You have for
me so that I don't end up outside of
all You have prepared for my future.

LUKE 13:24-25

This is what I'm led to pray as I read God's Word today.

The Scripture I have read is _____.

_____

_____

_____

_____

_____

_____

_____

_____

_____

_____

_____

_____

_____

_____

_____

_____

_____

Lord, pierce my conscience
whenever I am drawn toward anything
less than a humble attitude.

LUKE 14:11

This is what I'm led to pray as I read God's Word today.

The Scripture I have read is _____.

_____

_____

_____

_____

_____

_____

_____

_____

_____

_____

_____

_____

God, I pray that I will always be
faithful with the material possessions
You have given me, and that with them
I will serve and glorify only You.

LUKE 16:10-13

This is what I'm led to pray as I read God's Word today.

The Scripture I have read is _____.

_____

_____

_____

_____

_____

_____

_____

_____

_____

_____

_____

_____

_____

_____

_____

Heavenly Father, thank
You that You are a God who is moved by
persistent prayer and You hear me when
I cry out to You day and night. Because of
that I will always pray and not give up.

LUKE 18:1-8

This is what I'm led to pray as I read God's Word today.

The Scripture I have read is _____.

_____

_____

_____

_____

_____

_____

_____

_____

_____

_____

_____

_____

_____

_____

Lord, I thank You that because I
have received You and believe Your Word,
I will have everlasting life and death is
only a passage into life with You forever.

JOHN 5:24

This is what I'm led to pray as I read God's Word today.

The Scripture I have read is _____.

Jesus, You are the bread of heaven, and You give life to the world. I thank You that because I have come to You and received You, I will never hunger or thirst.

JOHN 6:32-35

This is what I'm led to pray as I read God's Word today.

The Scripture I have read is _____.

_____

_____

_____

_____

_____

_____

_____

_____

_____

_____

_____

_____

_____

God, help me never to speak for
my own glory but for Your glory only.

JOHN 7:18

This is what I'm led to pray as I read God's Word today.

The Scripture I have read is _____.

_____

_____

_____

_____

_____

_____

_____

_____

_____

_____

_____

_____

_____

_____

_____

_____

Dear Jesus, I thank
You that You are the door through which
I can enter and find salvation, security,
provision, and abundance of life.

JOHN 10:9-10

This is what I'm led to pray as I read God's Word today.

The Scripture I have read is _____.

_____

_____

_____

_____

Jesus, thank You that You are the light of the world. Because I walk with You, I will never have to live in darkness.

JOHN 12:46

This is what I'm led to pray as I read God's Word today.

The Scripture I have read is _____.

_____

_____

_____

_____

_____

_____

_____

_____

_____

_____

_____

_____

_____

_____

_____

_____

Lord, help me to love
others the way You have loved
me and will always love me.

JOHN 13:34

This is what I'm led to pray as I read God's Word today.

The Scripture I have read is _____.

_____

Holy Spirit of God,
in Jesus' name I pray that You would
teach me all I need to know and
guide me in all things and into all truth.

JOHN 16:13

This is what I'm led to pray as I read God's Word today.

The Scripture I have read is _____.

_____

_____

_____

_____

_____

_____

_____

_____

_____

_____

_____

_____

_____

_____

_____

_____

Lord, my treasure is in You,
and I ask You to help me generously
share that treasure with others.

ACTS 3:6

This is what I'm led to pray as I read God's Word today.

The Scripture I have read is _____.

_____

_____

_____

_____

_____

_____

_____

_____

_____

_____

_____

_____

_____

_____

_____

_____

_____

_____

_____

Father God, keep me from ever being confused or influenced by the enemy so that I will never lie to You or anyone else.

ACTS 5:4

This is what I'm led to pray as I read God's Word today.

The Scripture I have read is _____.

Lord, enable me to
speak boldly about You and not
be silenced by the fear of man.

ACTS 18:9-10

This is what I'm led to pray as I read God's Word today.

The Scripture I have read is _____.

_____

_____

_____

_____

_____

_____

_____

_____

_____

_____

_____

_____

_____

_____

_____

_____

_____

Thank You, Lord,
that even though I have sinned and
fallen short of all You have for me,
You still love me and lead me on
the path You want me to walk.
ROMANS 3:23

This is what I'm led to pray as I read God's Word today.

The Scripture I have read is _____.

_____

_____

_____

_____

_____

_____

_____

_____

_____

_____

_____

_____

_____

_____

_____

Heavenly Father,
I am grateful that even in hard times I
can feel Your love, and You are always
working in me a greater sense of hope.

ROMANS 5:3-5

This is what I'm led to pray as I read God's Word today.

The Scripture I have read is _____.

_____

_____

_____

_____

_____

_____

_____

_____

_____

_____

_____

_____

_____

_____

_____

_____

_____

_____

God, help me to be in Your
Word and to understand it so that
I will grow in faith every day.

ROMANS 10:17

This is what I'm led to pray as I read God's Word today.

The Scripture I have read is _____.

Lord, help me to always
remember that I am the temple
of Your Holy Spirit so that I never
treat my body carelessly.

1 CORINTHIANS 3:16-17

This is what I'm led to pray as I read God's Word today.

The Scripture I have read is _____.

_____

_____

_____

_____

_____

_____

_____

_____

_____

_____

_____

_____

_____

_____

_____

_____

_____

Enable me to always glorify
You in my body and spirit, Lord, and
to stay completely free of any kind of
inappropriate thoughts or actions.

1 CORINTHIANS 6:18

This is what I'm led to pray as I read God's Word today.

The Scripture I have read is _____.

_____

_____

_____

_____

_____

_____

_____

_____

_____

_____

_____

_____

_____

_____

_____

_____

_____

Thank You, Jesus,
that because of the power of Your
Spirit in me, I can never be tempted
beyond my ability to resist.

I CORINTHIANS 10:12-13

This is what I'm led to pray as I read God's Word today.

The Scripture I have read is _____.

_____

Help me, Lord, to bring every
thought under godly control and to be
entirely submitted to obeying You.

2 CORINTHIANS 10:3-5

This is what I'm led to pray as I read God's Word today.

The Scripture I have read is _____.

_____

_____

_____

_____

_____

_____

_____

_____

_____

_____

_____

_____

_____

_____

_____

_____

_____

Dear Lord, enable
me to resist futile thoughts and blindness
of heart so that I can be renewed in
my mind and live the righteous and
holy life You have called me to live.
EPHESIANS 4:22-24

This is what I'm led to pray as I read God's Word today.

The Scripture I have read is _____.

_____

_____

_____

_____

_____

_____

_____

_____

_____

_____

_____

_____

_____

_____

_____

_____

Jesus, teach me to love others
the way You do so that I don't say or do
anything out of selfishness or pride.

PHILIPPIANS 2:3-4

This is what I'm led to pray as I read God's Word today.

The Scripture I have read is _____.

_____

_____

_____

_____

_____

_____

_____

_____

_____

_____

_____

_____

_____

_____

_____

_____

_____

Heavenly Father,
I pray that You would open doors for
me to speak of Your greatness
to others and give me the
perfect words to say at all times.
COLOSSIANS 4:2-5

This is what I'm led to pray as I read God's Word today.

The Scripture I have read is _____.

_____

_____

_____

_____

_____

_____

_____

_____

_____

_____

_____

_____

_____

_____

_____

_____

_____

_____

Dear God, put in my
heart an unfailing love for Your truth
so that I will never be deceived.

2 THESSALONIANS 2:9-10

This is what I'm led to pray as I read God's Word today.

The Scripture I have read is _____.

_____

_____

_____

_____

_____

_____

_____

_____

_____

_____

_____

_____

_____

_____

_____

God, help me to be disciplined
in my mind, body, and soul for Your
glory, and to always seek godliness as
a priority over anything else in life.

1 TIMOTHY 4:8

This is what I'm led to pray as I read God's Word today.

The Scripture I have read is _____.

_____

_____

_____

_____

_____

_____

_____

_____

_____

_____

_____

_____

_____

_____

_____

_____

Dear Jesus, give
me the words to tell people of the
good things in me because of You, and
help me share my faith with others
in a powerful and effective way.
PHILEMON 1:6

This is what I'm led to pray as I read God's Word today.

The Scripture I have read is _____.

_____

_____

_____

_____

_____

_____

_____

_____

_____

_____

_____

_____

_____

_____

_____

_____

_____

Jesus, help me to be in church
when I need to be and to always have
words of hope, love, and encouragement
for others when I see them.

HEBREWS 10:23-25

This is what I'm led to pray as I read God's Word today.

The Scripture I have read is _____.

Lord, I submit myself to
Your control and pray that every word
coming out of my mouth will glorify You
and bring blessing and life to others.

JAMES 3:8-10

This is what I'm led to pray as I read God's Word today.

The Scripture I have read is _____.

_____

_____

_____

_____

_____

_____

_____

_____

_____

_____

_____

_____

_____

_____

_____

_____

Lord, help me to never
return for even a moment to the things
from which You have delivered me.

2 PETER 2:20-21

This is what I'm led to pray as I read God's Word today.

The Scripture I have read is _____.

_____

_____

_____

_____

_____

_____

_____

_____

_____

_____

_____

_____

_____

_____

_____

Help me to always remember, Lord, that Your Spirit in me is greater than anything I face.

I JOHN 4:4

This is what I'm led to pray as I read God's Word today.

The Scripture I have read is _____.

_____

_____

_____

_____

_____

_____

_____

_____

_____

_____

_____

_____

_____

_____

_____

_____

_____

_____

_____

_____

Help me, Lord, to show
my love for You by always living
according to Your commands.

2 JOHN 1:6

This is what I'm led to pray as I read God's Word today.

The Scripture I have read is _____.

_____

_____

_____

_____

_____

_____

_____

_____

_____

_____

_____

_____

_____

_____

_____

_____

_____

Heavenly Father,
help me to prosper in all things and enjoy
good health in my body, mind, and soul.

3 JOHN 1:2

This is what I'm led to pray as I read God's Word today.

The Scripture I have read is _____.

_____

_____

_____

_____

_____

_____

_____

_____

_____

_____

_____

_____

_____

_____

_____

_____

Thank You, Jesus,
that You are able to keep me from
stumbling and falling and to present
me before God without any fault.

JUDE 1:24

This is what I'm led to pray as I read God's Word today.

The Scripture I have read is _____.

_____

_____

_____

_____

_____

_____

_____

_____

_____

_____

_____

_____

_____

_____

_____

Jesus, I pray that I will never
lose the fervency of love for You that
I should have and that You deserve.

REVELATION 2:4-5

This is what I'm led to pray as I read God's Word today.

The Scripture I have read is _____.

_____

_____

_____

_____

_____

_____

_____

_____

_____

_____

_____

_____

_____

_____

_____

_____

Thank You, Jesus,
that I can overcome the enemy by the
power of Your blood shed for me.

REVELATION 12:10-12

This is what I'm led to pray as I read God's Word today.

The Scripture I have read is _____.

_____

_____

_____

_____

_____

_____

_____

_____

_____

_____

_____

_____

_____

_____

Lord, thank You that You
make all things new, and one day I will
be with You and there will be no more
death or sorrow or pain or tears.

REVELATION 21:4-5